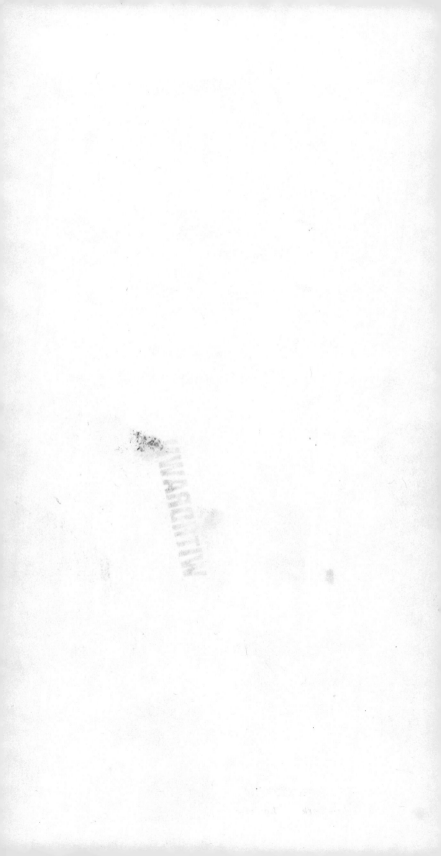

Soft Hay will Catch you

POEMS BY YOUNG PEOPLE

Compiled by Sandford Lyne

Illustrated by Julie Monks

SIMON & SCHUSTER BOOKS FOR YOUNG READERS

New York   London   Toronto   Sydney

SIMON & SCHUSTER BOOKS FOR YOUNG READERS

An imprint of Simon & Schuster Children's Publishing Division

1230 Avenue of the Americas, New York, New York 10020

Compilation copyright © 2004 by Sandford Lyne

Illustrations copyright © 2004 by Julie Monks

Excerpt from *The Radiant Child* by Thomas Armstrong, reprinted by permission of the author; quote from page 31 used as epigraph from *Eternal Echoes: Exploring Our Yearning to Belong* by John O'Donohue, copyright © 1999 by John O'Donohue, reprinted by permission of HarperCollins Publishers Inc.; excerpt from *Timely Rain: Selected Poetry of Chogyam Trungpa,* copyright © 1972, 1983, 1998 by Diana J. Mukpo, reprinted by arrangement with Shambhala Publications, Inc., Boston, www.shambhala.com; excerpt from *Kiss of God* by Marshall Stewart Ball, reprinted by permission of the author.

SIMON & SCHUSTER BOOKS FOR YOUNG READERS is a trademark of Simon & Schuster, Inc.

Book design by Greg Stadnyk

The text for this book is set in Bembo.

The illustrations are rendered in oil paints.

Manufactured in the United States of America

10 9 8 7 6 5 4 3 2 1

Library of Congress Cataloging-in-Publication Data

Soft hay will catch you : poems by young people / compiled by

Sandford Lyne ; illustrations by Julie Monks.

p. cm.

Includes index.

Summary: A collection of poems written by young people aged eight to eighteen on a variety of subjects.

ISBN 0-689-83460-8

1. Children's poetry, American. 2. Children's writings, American.

[1. American poetry—Collections. 2. Children's writings. 3. Youth's writings.] I. Lyne, Sandford. II. Monks, Julie, ill.

PS586.3.S64 2004

811.008'09282—dc21

2003005978

To my heroes, the classroom teachers
—S. L.

For S. B.
—J. M.

CONTENTS

ACKNOWLEDGMENTS

My "barter trip" back to Kentucky in 1994 to teach a poetry-writing workshop in exchange for the opportunity to stay with relatives on their farms happily has become an annual event, the kickoff to my school year of travel and teaching. My special thanks to Becky and Jerry McKinney, and Charles Mac Noe and Mary Nelle Noe, for their warm hospitality, and to all the staff and faculty at Adairville School for making this possible. My heartfelt thanks to Lew Tilford and Jeanne Averill and the Lawrence (KS) Public Schools, Terry Boyer and Mercantile Bank of Lawrence, The Lied Center of the University of Kansas, and the business community of Lawrence for inviting me to help design and present a five-year program to introduce poetry writing systemwide in the Lawrence schools as part of their "Adventures in Imagination" literacy program; to Barbara Shepherd, Amy Duma, and the John F. Kennedy Center for the Performing Arts education programs and their numerous partnerships nationwide—especially The Wang Center in Boston, the Maui Arts & Cultural Center in Kahului, Black Liberated Arts in Oklahoma City, and Columbus (IN) Area Arts Council—for providing me a wide forum for my work with teachers; to the many schools across the country that invited me to present poetry workshops to students; to Faye King and Stanton (KY) Elementary for their inspiration in using the arts (bluegrass music) to build school community; to Pam Weinantz of Wheatfields (Columbus, IN) for her vision of using the arts in a rural setting for education and healing; to the Acadiana Arts Council and Jeff Davis Arts Council for their financial support for workshops in Louisiana; to my friend Sandy LaBry for being the muse and beacon to guide me to my new home in Louisiana; and to my sister, Jayn Stewart, and Carol Beau, Nancy Morgan, Lance Brunner, Renée Roberts, Karen Shrode, Jacie Huber, Harriet Maher, Dr. Sally Dobyns, Dr. Ann Dobie, Ellen and Tim Collins, and so many other friends and colleagues whose kindnesses and support made my work with students and teachers possible.

INTRODUCTION

My parents were part of that remarkable generation who went from the horse and buggy to the walk on the moon, embracing more change than any generation in history. They knew a life of farms and small towns, which gave them a love of simple things—friendships, family gatherings, jokes, stories, needed rains, plentiful crops and summer vegetables, a big porch (I could go on and on), and, of course, the beauties of the natural world (pastures, fields, woods, lakes, rivers, and ponds). It was a love that they passed on to me—a love not for things, but for *experiences*. They were not the kind of parents who sit a child down and drive home a pointed lesson, but their personal integrity, generosity, fairness, and kindness, and their deep and consistent pleasure with the shared human experience—more often than not conveyed only with the warmth of their eyes, their smiles—added the first quiet brushstrokes of depth to my own learning and understanding.

My mother believed it was important to read to me—until I could read for myself. She noticed my interests (they were fortunately inexpensive interests, such as drawing) and happily bought me things I needed to pursue them (drawing tablets, pencils, charcoal, and drawing pens and ink). Not an artist herself, she left entirely up to me what I drew and how I used my imagination. I think she saw her role as the guardian and supplier of my means and opportunities.

Not only the guardian of *my* interests and opportunities, my mother was also a classroom teacher; she taught eighth-grade math and ninth-grade Latin at one of our local schools, and she was my teacher for both (and I learned to finish my homework just at bedtime, so she would not—in her enthusiasm for those subjects—give me more to do!). Even in this setting, at school, my mother's most profound instruction almost always came indirectly, often without her knowing. I remember a particular Monday when I was in the eighth grade. Over the weekend a man had been arrested in our town for trying to rob a grocery store. The story was in the Sunday paper, and everyone seemed to know about it. The man's son went to my school, and during the day he had been taunted unmercifully. Students said things to that boy in the halls like "Your daddy's a dirty, no-good robber" and "Your daddy's a jailbird." At the end of the day I went to my mother's classroom to meet her for the ride home. The door, almost always open, was closed. I opened it slowly and quietly. At the front of the room I saw my mother at her desk with her head in her hands. She was crying, not loud, but I could hear her sobs.

"What's wrong?" I asked. Lifting her head and

wiping her eyes with a tissue, she told me that she knew the man who robbed the grocery store. He had a wife and three children. She told me that he had very little education, that he was a good person and hardworking. She said she knew he had been out of work for months, unable to find a job, only finding a little yard work here and there. She said she thought he must have been desperate to feed his family, or he wouldn't have done such a thing. She felt sad for the man, and for his family, and for his son who had been the brunt of cruel remarks that day.

I stood there in silence, taking in what my mother was saying. With those heartfelt tears and a few words, she was teaching me a lifetime lesson—to suspend judgment and to look below the surface of things, to wonder at the whole story of each person in the world before making up one's mind about them. The poet Ralph Waldo Emerson wrote, "Every smile and every tear deserves a history."

My mother's death in 1992 took my sister and me back to Kentucky. It was my first trip back to see my relatives in almost twenty years. Almost all of them are farmers in Logan County, and they told my sister and me how much they loved my mother, and talked about her quiet sense of humor, and about how much they missed her after she retired and moved east to be near her grandchildren. For me it was a time to connect with memories of a childhood visiting these farms and farmers—feeding chickens with my great-aunt and climbing about in the lofts of barns with my cousins. I remembered a ride one afternoon through fields and woods on the back of a horse with my mother to see the one-room schoolhouse where she first taught when she was only eighteen years old.

It was on this return trip that I also made a special connection with a cousin, Becky McKinney, who is a third-grade teacher in the K-to-8 school in nearby Adairville. We talked about my work as a poet-teacher, traveling across the United States to teach poetry writing to young people and training their teachers in creative writing. Becky said she wished her students could have an experience like that. And so we struck a deal, a "barter." I would come back to teach a one-week poetry-writing workshop in exchange for the rich and simple pleasure of staying with relatives on their farms.

The following September I returned, staying with Becky's parents: kind, generous, salt-of-the-earth farmers. The first morning I drove to school along a two-lane road that rose and fell over gently curving hills, the fields lush with ripened corn and soybeans and ready-to-cut tobacco, a white-silver mist in places low to the ground. There were cattle out in the open and under the trees, huge red and black barns, ponds as blue as cornflowers, and the smoky-sweet scent of curing tobacco in the air. By the time I reached the school I was intoxicated with the sights and smells, and walking into the first classroom, the words tumbled out, "My gosh, you kids live in paradise!"

"Paradise?" The students looked stunned. They thought I couldn't mean it, this poet to whom they might be distantly related, this stranger whose parents lived where they lived but who himself lived in Washington, D.C., the nation's capital. It seemed to them that they lived at the ends of the earth, in the boondocks, nowhere.

But I had learned a long time ago to look beneath the surface of things and to believe in the treasures and lessons hidden in each life, to believe in the history of each smile and tear. As a poet myself, I knew that my own world of images and metaphors was grown in the deep topsoil and in the seed experiences of my childhood, sometimes in the very places where these students now walked and lived. I knew that a fact learned by walking a field is not the same fact found only in a book or on the Internet, and that writing, which is inward listening, adds something else to the fact, adds to the fact the deeper mystery of the Self. This mystery and its appearance is not something that can be explained; it must be experienced. Trusting in this mystery, Emerson again wrote, "Every writer is a skater, and must go partly where he would, and partly where the skates take him." With patience, the possibilities before us were rich indeed. Mia Payne, a fourth grader I had worked with, writing about a walk through a wild field to a pond, ended her poem with just such an awakened awareness:

It was slower to my feet,
but faster to my heart.

And so, together, we got on "the slow horse of poetry" to ride out on the roads and landscapes of their personal stories. I became the guardian and supplier of means and opportunities; they did the rest. Over the course of the week they began to write poems about fields of corn, soybeans, and tobacco, about cattle and tractors and creeks and hills and barns, about their mamas and daddies, their aunts and uncles and cousins. They wrote about loneliness and solitude, about loss and recovery, sometimes turning a sorrow into sentences of transcendent beauty. They discovered— as I knew they would—that the poems they wrote were the "histories" of their own smiles, their own tears. And on the last day one boy looked up at me, his face illumined by the words of his own poems, and—speaking for himself and many of his classmates—the words came tumbling out, "Mr. Lyne, you were right. We do live in paradise."

The Inward Fire

Poems About the Search for the Self

There are two sides to the developing child.
One side is busy adapting to the contours of
the three-dimensional world. The other side is
at work remembering divine origins.

—THOMAS ARMSTRONG
THE RADIANT CHILD

I run from
the shadows and sounds
But sometimes I find the courage
within me
to explore the darkness
And
there I
find
myself

—Manuel Dawson
Grade 5

MY QUIET PLACE

Lying on the bed of leaves
from the naked tree above
I let my mind drift away in silence
a silence so strong
I can hear the steady thump
of my own beating heart
as I stare up at the darkening sky
dreaming lazily about the past
about villains and pirates
and if I was one
would I be smart enough to find
the X that marked the spot of the treasure

—ASHLEE RUST
Grade 7

SUPERIOR

One day I went to show my friends
my new silver-coated bike.
They admired me and my bike, especially
how I raced down a path of stone.
They praised me like I was a god.
Oh how much I loved that moment.
I couldn't bear the thought of leaving it.

—ALPHA KILFU
Grade 5

THE SECRETS

People are forests
with many hidden glories.
Few people look deep enough
past the thick wood
past the dense fog
and into the marsh
where the buzzing insects may be heard
passing the inward secrets.

—BRETT WARNER
Grade 6

INNOCENCE

His boyhood was gone;
his manhood was just beginning.
The shade of the trees,
the birdsongs at his side,
sheltered him from the world.
Deep inside himself
he knew he must go,
but not yet, not just yet.

—DANIELLE COTNER
Grade 6

SILENCE

During my childhood,
I disliked my silence.
I wanted to be like the other girls,
singing dancing evermore.

—My-Ha Moon
Grade 5

THE TIDES

I walk along the ocean's edge
my toes curling in the sand
My heart feels its tides
their burning power
their amazing depth
I shut my eyes and close my heart
I am not ready for their power

—KELLY LEIGH HAFER
Grade 6

I live on a
mountain of coal
my friend lives with me
his name is Jeremy Back
well me and him
do the same thing and
we have the same face.

—JUSTIN HORN
Grade 5

SHADOWS LURK

Shadows lurk all
around me, scaring
me as they merrily
dance in little columns,
trying to prove they're
boss, but they won't
hold me back, for I'm
much more powerful
than they.

—BRENNA LAYNE STEBBINS
Grade 6

WILD

As I was walking through the forest on
a hot summer day,
I felt an outburst of energy.
I felt like I was as free as a dream
and climbed every tree and stone.
I couldn't stop.
Something inside me had trapped me
in a world of wildness.

—MICHAEL BLANK
Grade 6

MY KNIGHT

During class,
I wander off in my imagination.
I become the knight in shining armor
and slay the fearsome dragon.
Then with blood on my sword
and rust on my helmet
I become myself again,
back in class.

—ANDREW SCHREIBMAN
Grade 6

DIFFERENT WORLDS

Different worlds,
one in leaf,
one in flame.
It seemed that one world
was holding me back
from the other.
But not that day.
Off in the distance
I could see adulthood.

—ELIZABETH THOMPSON
Grade 5

ME

As I sit
in my Aunt Sue's
soft lap,
I grip the hard rubber
of her old
brown Chevy's
steering wheel.
I look up
and halfway smile.
I think I'm driving,
but everyone knows I'm not.

—CHRIS RAMSEY
Grade 7

KENTUCKY DANCE

Oh, I'm one of those restless cowboy girls
who rides horses,
who dances for those cute boys.
I'm restless.
I'm plain too,
but the boys clap for me!

—VIOLET MILLER
Grade 4

THE DARE

Today, today is the day I do the dare,
the dare to climb the ladder to the loft.
Today I must climb the ladder
with no hay on the ground
to cushion my fall.
I have been dreading this day for so long!
I have tried to get out of this,
but now I must go to the barn.

—COLLIN O'BRIEN
Grade 4

THE ECHO

Through the pines
my echo booms.
It seems to shake
the sun it sounds
so loud.
I yell and yell,
not minding the
branches that scratch
my arms and legs,
for I am acting as
myself and that is
all that matters.

—MEAGAN PADGETT
Grade 5

17

INTEGRITY

Keep going, I tell myself, alone in my rowboat.
A full moon flanks me in the dark,
making reflections like little candles
against the soft, dark water.

—BRYCE YOUNG
Grade 7

INWARD FLAME

As I awake,
I feel the gentle hand of Spring.
In a far-off place,
I hear the never-ending song of the sparrow,
a place deep in my soul.
It touches me,
like a roaring fire in winter,
like my inward flame.

—BEN LOWENKRON
Grade 5

my Fire casts shadows

Poems About Solitude and Loneliness

A faithful friend is the
medicine of life.

—ECCLESIASTICUS

Nothing can bring you
peace but yourself.

—RALPH WALDO EMERSON

THE LONELY FIRE

The fire is lonely.
Its flame dances
in the evening wind.
The art of the lonely fire
is soothing to my soul.
Dance on, lonely fire.

—MICHAEL J. WEILER
Grade 4

LONESOME

I sit in my narrow pirogue
deep in the desolate swamp,
the cooling rain
sprinkling my weathered face.
I am so hungry my stomach
is tied in knots,
and I wish
someone was with me to see
the colors of nature.

—DAVID W. DUGUEANT JR.
Grade 12

HIGH ISLAND

I walk along the rocky coast.
Its round rocks hurt my bare feet,
and still I walk on,
enduring the pain,
realizing that what I see
is far more valuable
than what I feel.

—JOHN H. BLACKSTEN
Grade 10

LONELINESS

I sit against an old oak tree.
As the chill of the wind hits me,
the leaves glide gently to the ground.
A tear falls from my cheek,
and I feel lost.
Children are playing beyond the trees
of the enchanted forest.
They stare.
They talk.
They whisper and tease,
but I am alone and afraid
of what would happen to me
if I joined them.

—BESS TUCKER
Grade 5

RUMORS

It is summer.
I look over at the older boys
by the creaky bench.
I go over to them
and hear them telling secrets.
I ask them to tell me one.
The boys say yes.
I have a bunch of joy run through me.
Then all the joy goes away.
The rumor is about me.

—AARON D. BERNDSTON
Grade 4

MAD

I hate those other boys.
They make me so mad.
The new rule says
I have to play with them.
I have a dark heart.
I stand alone in cold.
I am nothing but
mad.

—CHASE FRIEL
Grade 4

REJECTED

My friend crossed the creek
without me that morning.
Oh how much I wanted to be a rainbow
full of bright colors
so I would be noticed.
But instead I was a girl,
just a girl.

—Elizabeth Thompson
Grade 5

A LONELY DAY

The dragonfly flies silently
over the still pond,
his face expressionless.
I wonder,
has he ever cried?

—BRET ROBINSON
Grade 6

LITTLE TEARS

Her tears drop on my shoulder
and drown out the laughter.
If I could get the laughter back,
all would be better.

—BRIDGET FAE HEDMAN
Grade 6

There have been mirages in the road
for hours. Even my dog cowers.

—MATTHEW BOEHM
Grade 3

BLACKBIRDS

I sat in the tall, green grass.
The rain and thunder didn't bother me.
I didn't mind that there was no one there
    to talk to
as long as the blackbirds didn't leave.

—EMILY KING
Grade 6

NEW KID

There is a new kid
on the block.
He chases dragonflies
by the pond.
I think silently
should I play with him.
God tells me
go and play with him
to start the kindness
of another day.

—MATTHEW SCHNALL
Grade 3

ALONE FOREVER

I am alone, alone forever.
I hear silence
every day and night.
I feel like I am going in circles.
I sometimes feel like firewood
burning in an open field,
like a broken window
by itself in a room.
One day,
I will have enough faith and hope
to just stop being
alone forever.

—ASHLEY SANDERS
Grade 6

WAITING

I am lonely today, sitting
barefoot by the gleaming lake,
waiting for my father
to come through the trees.
The sun is starting to set
into the horizon, herons flying,
getting dark. Soon I hope
my father comes behind
the shadows of the oak trees.

—RICHARD MOORE
Grade 7

Many days go by,
yet it seems so slow.
Many times I'm alone,
but really I'm among many.
When I fall,
it will end with grace.
When I go down,
someone will be there
to praise.

—BRIAN FORMAN
Grade 6

OUT MY WINDOW

I am alone today.
I look out my window with an empty heart
and see a red fox in the beautiful mist.
He also has an empty heart,
but he catches a great fish
in the reeds for his dawn snack.

—DANA BARNEY
Grade 5

Walking up the dunes,
legs grow tired, thoughts drift
to other places,
only to be brought into unity again
by the sight of empty perfection
rolling towards shore.

—RICHARD FURST
Grade 10

smoke and embers
Poems About the Home and Family

A home . . . is the cradle of one's future. Home is the place where the stranger arrives . . . the place where you see things for the first time. Here you first begin to know that you have a body . . . different gifts are being quietly received by each member of the family. Gifts that will take a full lifetime to unwrap and recognize.

—JOHN O'DONOHUE
ETERNAL ECHOES

PAPPY

My grandfather gently gathers my hair in his hand
   to sweep it away from my face.
He asks me to tell him my troubles, for which his
   love will be my strength.
A spring breeze invisibly brushes buttercups
   into streams of lasting sun.

—GEORGIA GROFF
Grade 11

PICTURED MOMENT

A fallen tree
leaning on another.
My brother, further up than I.
He was always first.
I always followed.
I would try anything he did.
Termites and black ants
were walking on my hands.
My brother tried to go higher.
I stared at the ground.
Knees shaking, bladder weak.
I wanted to get down,
but I stayed on, clutching the tree,
scraping my knees.
I would do anything he did.

—KARINA CHRISTENSEN
Grade 11

MY DAD

My dad rides in the combine,
smiling so sweet.
Though I can tell he's hungry and tired,
I know he'll have room for me.
I'll sit right by his feet.
We'll talk about many things.
Who knows? Maybe not.
We might go home in an hour.
Maybe even five.
Who knows?
But who cares?
The longer the time,
the more I get to know him.

—MARY ZAUNBRECHER
Grade 7

MOM'S GUMBO

As my mom started to make
the roux for the gumbo,
a butterfly flew in the room.
Suddenly there was a terrible rain,
washing the air clean.
The room filled with a silver light,
shining from the levee.
And at last, the gumbo was ready.

—HOLLY DENNIS
Grade 4

THE HUNT

Walking home from hunting
with my kill in my vest,
listening to the owl
sing its song,
walking across the field looking
at the dark woods behind me,
looking at the moon
in the sky as I walk.
In the distance I see
a far-off light of a car
coming down the field road.
As I come upon my house,
my dad sits on the porch
waiting for me to come home.
As I get there, he asks me
if I killed anything.
I throw him my vest, and he
says, "I guess so."

—JOEY ABSHIRE
Grade 7

STORY IN THE GRASS

One day Grandma took me to the park
and set me in the grass.
She told me a story of soldiers fighting.
They were hurt so badly they slept
forever deep in the ground.
Grandma called them dead.
She told me Grandpa was one of them,
and we both cried for a reason
I didn't quite understand.

—CARLY CROSS
Grade 10

MOTHER

My mom sits with her jewels on.
A web of makeup spreads across her face.
Dad works on the fence outside,
and it's about to rain.

—C. J. HORNBROOK
Grade 3

A FATHER'S MIND

I have a daughter who likes boys.
She would like to rule
them every year;
and when her heart breaks,
I'm always there
yelling at the boy.
Through the breeze,
I can see the boys lining up.
They look like a storm
lining up for her.

—CHRIS BROCKELMAN
Grade 7

FATHER'S WORK

Father is starting work
at sunrise.
He'll bring his hoe
and an apple.
Father's work
ends at sundown.
He'll return home
with shadows
at his sides.

—KELLY MILLER
Grade 4

A SUNSET

As I mothered my growing sunflowers,
evening fell upon me.
I was suddenly startled by the slam
of the screen door.
Father was home.
Mom came outside to fetch me;
her silky, smooth hands
pushed my hair behind my ear.
She drew me inside as the last gleam
of sunshine faded into the darkness.

—SAIRA KHAN
Grade 5

MY MOTHER'S BOAT

As the river flows,
colors from the sky lie upon it.
My mother's boat falls asleep,
and knots in the wood disappear.
As she stares into her worn hands,
her expression changes.
Memories appear from
the deepest folds of her palms.

—SARA CAREY-PROCK
Grade 7

COMING HOME LATE

Late evening. I'm walking
down a gravel road past cow
pastures. I see dark, black
oak trees. I look up and see
the Big and Little Dippers.
I come to my driveway and see
the porch light on. I get
to the door and see my dad
sitting on the swing of
the front porch, worried
about where I was. He
says, "Shhh, your mother
fell asleep on the couch."

—REBEKAH M. HEBERT
Grade 6

SILENCE

The sun is shining brightly
on the stillness
of the grass.
I hear a small voice.
It sounds like Mother's.
I think she's calling me for
our first supper without Father.

—JESSICA AUSTIN
Grade 6

SAD

I'm sad
when I see
children with their grandparents.

I'm sad
when I see
kids with two parents,
not one.

I'm sad
when I see
what I've missed.

—LYNNE SCHWARZER
Grade 6

MY ROLE

I now have an important
role in my house,
sometimes hard, sometimes easy.
My role is to be
man of the house.
I know this is
a big man's job and
when one comes,
he can take over.

—WILLIAM KAVANAUGH
Grade 6

ABSENCE

Her father was like the wind,
journeying any and everywhere.
As a small girl, she only saw her father
in her dreams.
She'd sit under that tree
by the stream and praise his name—
the father she did not know.

—LINDSAY INGRAM
Grade 7

ALL WORK NO PLAY

I've worked all day
and now my body is full of hurt.
My father says you have to work
to make a living.
Now as the sun goes down
I think about today.
He didn't make me work
so I would be mad.
He made me work so I could make
more out of my life.
That's why I got to drive the tractor.
That's why I got to hammer the nails.
And now as I settle down for bed
I pray for my father.

—Jacob Kucza
Grade 6

GRANDFATHER'S TALES

As I sit on my grandfather's lap,
I listen to his intriguing tales.
He talks of when he was a warrior
and hunted bison on the flat mesas.
I think he misses those days,
but now he can relive them,
telling stories to his grandchild.

—SUZY ALLEN
Grade 6

The World of Dew
Poems About the Soul's Journey and the Circle of Life

The child's world has no beginning or end.
To him, colors are neither beautiful nor ugly.
The child's nature has no preconceived notion
   of birth and death.

—CHOGYAM TRUNGPA

THE MORNING SHORE

I stand in the coastal breeze
The sky blooms
starting from east to west
slowly depleting
the pure, white stars
in the dawn sky.

—CILTON VILLEMARETTE III
Grade 9

THE FOX

A red flash went flying
through the mist.
I was out at dawn.
The air was so sweet then.
I heard an owl getting ready to sleep.
The fox became one spirit of the earth
instead of two spirits of the world.

—BRITTON M. REID
Grade 3

THE ANGEL

In the courtyard,
I am being watched by angels.
They are watching me, protecting me,
and I feel safe.
In the center of the courtyard,
there is a stone angel, a different one,
and she is me.
I sit by the fountain and watch the angel.
She is frozen there, silent, just like me.
And though neither of us says anything,
she absorbs my unspoken troubles
which are not unlike her own.

—MARY KATE HAWORTH
Grade 7

SHADOWS OF THE SUN

As I stand here with my artwork,
I see someone in the hot summer light
heading straight for the sun
on a never-ending path.
I can still see the shadow of her
waiting for me to come too.

—CAMILLE MYERS
Grade 5

DANCING AND SINGING

Underneath the sycamore tree,
the river flows gently.
Up above, you can hear
the loud rumbling
of the gods and angels,
dancing and singing
to
the tune of the river
and wind!

—MARGO CALDWELL
Grade 5

A DIFFERENT PLACE

I'm moving away from all my friends.
I'm moving to a different place.
I'm going to live on a different street,
in a different house, in that different place.
Everything will be different but the moon.
The moon will follow us wherever we go.

—HELEN VASALY
Grade 5

THE LAST TIME I CAN SEE

On the boat heading to sea.
Look back. My entire country behind me.
The boat shoving forward, and up, down
with the waves and wind.
The whole scene of shore, forest
slowly fades and shrinks.
The boat moves further.
My heart beats faster.

—MINH TRAN
Grade 12

DAY'S END

The sun waves good-bye.
The waters of life slowly stop.
The shadowy sky moves in.
You can only hear your breath
against eons of stillness.

—SARAH SAJEWSKI
Grade 5

Flip Flop is with me
My sorrow grows
for Flip Flop's death is coming
She is old
her Siamese is going
If she dies
a part of me dies too

—MICHELLE HARRIS
Grade 8

I WISH MY DAYS WERE PEACEFUL

I wish my days were peaceful,
just like the simple sun's.
I wish my mind was clear,
just like the afternoon sky.
I wish my life was flowing,
just like a wondrous poem.
I wish my sinless angel would
come down and get me,
just like Grandpa's.

—STEPHANIE S. ZVONKOVICH
Grade 6

THE LADDER IN THE HAY

I was in the barn one day
when I found a ladder.
The ladder led to heaven.
I started to climb.
As I went up, I saw all my faults.
When I could not take it anymore,
I climbed down.
I buried the ladder back in the hay,
where someone else will find it one day.

—COLLEEN BRANIGAN
Grade 4

ALONE

I'm all alone in a churchyard.
Someone died today.
It was my friend,
my only friend.
His soul is wiped clean.
I am all alone, all alone.
The bell of his death rings.
His soul is white.
The boys that used to play with him
think it's no big deal.
My heart's breaking.
The breeze blows my hair.
He was always fair.
The rules he played by
were drawn to everyone's consent.
The tears roll down my cheeks.
My heart leaps into the sky
with sadness, then drops
like coins leaving someone's hand
and falling to the ground.

—ERICA HUNTER
Grade 4

A BREEZE

A June breeze goes over a field
In that field
there is a grave
which is empty
empty of the pleasures
of the sunrise
or the fountain in the park.

—ALEX APPLEMAN
Grade 5

A TIME TO CRY

I am sad
I hide in the house
I am sad
because my grandma died
and there is a bowl I see
I pick it up
I throw it out the window
and I cry
and I wipe
my tears off
with my sleeve.

—AUSTIN RAY MOORE
Grade 4

A DEATH

The truth has come,
and all hope has gone.
My tears outnumber the raindrops,
and heaven has opened its door.
My father, to me, was a gift,
an inspiration to the heart.
But now my dad has gone
to be with the other god.

—LIZ COLLINS
Grade 5

I am old,
but I can fit thousands of
beautiful stars in one
eye. I can see an angel
in a stream.
I can go back to my boyhood
and look for treasures with my dad.
I am old, but God is giving me strength.
I am tired,
but God is giving me energy,
and when I am too tired,
God will give me rest.

—LAWRENCE WHITE
Grade 6

A WONDERFUL PLACE

In my dreams I dream of a barn,
not just any barn,
a special barn.
When you go inside, a bright light shines,
and a ladder to heaven stands before you,
and if you fall—
no worry—
soft hay will catch you.

—CRYSTAL KIM
Grade 4

GOLDEN TRAILS

I took a walk
upon a road of glory,
through the fields
painted yellow gold,
to the insects by the pond
and in the pool.
It was slower to my feet,
but faster to my heart.

—MIA EMERALD PAYNE
Grade 4

Eternity's Sunrise

Poems About Awakenings and Discoveries

. . . he who kisses the joy as it flies
Lives in eternity's sun rise

—WILLIAM BLAKE
"ETERNITY"

Great is today, and beautiful,
It is good to live in this age . . . there never
was any better.

—WALT WHITMAN

A boy digs for stones,
A beautiful stone.
Not too big.
Not too small.
Not too shiny.
It has to be just right
to give this wonder
to his mother.

—BLAKE DEATHERAGE
Grade 4

POWER

The old man sits as if a king,
his crown the sun,
his cape the wind.
His shoulders are held comfortably,
a place of certainty.
I listen closely to his ideas;
they are like sparks for my fire.
As the beautiful afternoon turns dark,
he calls me into his palace,
for he wishes to dine.

—COOPER LANKFORD
Grade 7

LITTLE THINGS

I will remember for all
eternity looking into
that crow's eye,
the crow eating the
sunflower,
the crow picking at
my eye.
I will always
remember that
from this day forth.

—Ryan Shaughnessy
Grade 6

LIFE UNDER A
MICROSCOPE

Under the microscope,
an amazing world comes to life.
As I watch the amoeba
quickly surround its meal,
the slipperlike paramecium
slowly slithers in the distance.
The bacteria are scattering away
from the blinding light.
Could we be microorganisms
in the universe?

—CAITLIN USSELMAN
Grade 5

BEAUTY

The wind is strong,
but not as strong as beauty and love.
The wind blows the roses,
but there is love and beauty to hold
    them down.
You could have beauty all your life,
but love is how you got your beauty.

—CHARLES NWATU
Grade 5

ON THE FARM

The farm is still.
Cottonwoods are swaying.
A brilliant moonlit night this is,
and tonight our shadows combine.

—KRISTA HALEY
Grade 6

BEAUTY

I saw a poor girl
down swimming in the river.
I watched her long, knotty hair
sway back and forth.
It was the same magnificent
color as the sun.

—TEAL MEYER
Grade 6

BEWILDERMENT

I am bewildered.
God is the creator of all things,
as small as ants,
as big as elephants,
as miraculous as the moon.
But he still remembered to make me.

—DAVID ALLEN
Grade 3

SUMMER SHADOWS

As I walked down the forest path,
I saw the hot summer shadows
racing toward me,
covering me with woodland art.

—BRANDON MCANDERSON
Grade 6

SUMMER DANCE

As the music played on,
we danced in the orchard.
The theme tonight was love.
With the apples bright red
the sunset came low,
and the night danced in
for its long, black waltz.

—REGAN RAMP
Grade 6

RESTLESS

My favorite dance is any dance
where I dance with a girl.
I am restless to meet the one
that is right for me.
But I am just a plain 11-year-old boy
who looks as if he's 9.

—ROBERT BRYANT
Grade 6

INVITING RETURN

Evening.
I return from a long night of dancing.
Exhausted,
I climb the stairs and see
the candlelight through a crack in the door,
inviting me inside
to my cool, clean sheets.

—ALYCE LABRY
Grade 7

IT WON'T BE LONG

It won't be long
till I fall in love
with your willing touch
and your silent ways,
your sweet smile
and mysterious games.
It won't be long
till you open up to me.
Show me your heart
and I'll show you mine.
The world might move
or I'll move on,
but it won't be long.

—KRISTEN TEICHMANN
Grade 9

MOTH

The moth courts
the candle.
He courts it
in a flurry of wings.
He leaves
a little dust
on the piano.

—KIRSTEN LURIE HOFSTAD
Grade 5

THE QUIET SPIDER

The spider's on his web,
quiet as time,
hidden behind
the whitened
snow and
the green
pines.

—C. RYAN HOWARD
Grade 2

PEACEFUL

My mind is clear.
It is open to write a poem,
just as it is open to see an angel.

— MELISSA F. HARDY
Grade 6

THE POEM'S WAY

Poems have a way with me.
They love to tease my brain.
A small nibble is all I get,
for they have gone again
to the deepest, darkest spot
where even I,
the poet of the poem,
cannot reach.

—AARON TRENT
Grade 6

Green Words, Dancing Breezes

Poems About Our Connection to Place

I am made to love the pond and the meadow,
as the wind is made to ripple the water.

—HENRY DAVID THOREAU

Answers come when we are in our right place.

—MARSHALL STEWART BALL, *age 11*
FROM *KISS OF GOD*

THE MAGIC TOUCH

I cut through the cold blast of air
to the barn, warm with a herd of cows,
the white snow pounding me
with the blackness of winter.
I tread to the barn
and feed the newborn calves,
feeling their warm, rough tongues over
my bitterly cold hand.

—ANDREW MCKEE
Grade 6

BREATHING ROOM

I sit in an apple tree
far above the rolling cornfields
A nest of three blue eggs sits beside me
The golden leaves on the tree
rustle to a soft tune
The piece of hay in my mouth tastes
sweet and natural
as the autumn sun fades behind the clouds

—CHRISTINA SPELL
Grade 6

AUTUMN

The mules felt good
as the cool autumn wind
hit their sides
and the seeds of the trees
smacked them in the face.
Sheets of fog rose as it became
dusty dark.

—EARL MOBERLY
Grade 7

THE SEA OF CATTLE

The sea of horns seems to stretch endlessly.
Their white faces dot the ocean like salty brine.
Their hooves are like the roll of the thunderstorm
that tosses the dust into the air like salty spray.

—JON BERTRAND
Grade 11

THE GRAY IN BETWEEN

The blackness of night
and the whiteness of snow
meet as they settle upon the barn.
The white pushes up
and the dark pushes down.
The barn chooses no side;
it is devoured by both.

—LAURA K. HOLMAN
Grade 7

The day we moved
to our farm in Kansas
I was so sad,
but I went to our porch
and saw the coyote,
the deer and the hawk,
and I realized my new wealth.

—TRENT SANTEE
Grade 6

CUTTING BEANS

I drive through the field,
cutting my grandfather's beans.
The deer has left beautiful,
footed ruts. The horizon
strikes the corner of my eye.
How beautiful the Kansas sun.
As it begins to get dark,
the rows start to get smaller,
and I begin to get sleepy
and quit cutting
in my grandfather's
beautiful Kansas field.

—COLBY HARRELL
Grade 5

YEAR'S PAYCHECK

I am hauling my crop off today.
This is my favorite day
of the tobacco season.
I am afraid
that I will not get much money,
because the dogs ran through the crops
a thousand times a day
and knocked half the leaves off.
It is a rainy day.
I will have to throw a tarp over the tobacco
to keep it from ruining.
Last night I had a dream
that my crop would come in first place.
I doubt it, but I am ready
to collect my year's paycheck.

—ANDREW JOHNSON
Grade 7

IN THE FINAL HOURS OF SUNLIGHT

Final rays of sunlight glide over the horizon,
bringing the peaceful depths of darkness.
I lean back against the warping stable door,
fingering clumps of hay,
pressing the heel of my boot into the wet sawdust,
smelling the sweet scent of peppermint
from the warm air blowing from her nostrils,
lingering on the edge of a peaceful sleep,
savoring a perfect ride.

—JESSIE ANN KAUR GILL
Grade 8

BEAUTIFUL *AVE*

A beautiful *ave*
looks at me with its
shiny, *negros ojos,*
negro as space, *negro* as darkness.
The beautiful *ave*
ruffles its *plumas,*
soft as *las nubes.*
The beautiful *ave,*
its *plumas* are *brillantes.*
Brillante red,
like roses or *sangre.*
The beautiful *ave*
uses its spearlike *garras*
to move.
They are thin
like *palillos.*
The beautiful *ave* flying away
flies in the sky with its *alas.*
Almost like floating, *una burbuja,*
never to be seen again.

—REMON L. GINSBURG
Grade 12

A JOURNEY

The butterflies of summer have
gone to warmer fields.
The map they follow is not
of streets and smog, but rather
of trees, wind, sun,
and the smell of flowers.
In my mind, I migrate with them
to the high plateaus of Mexico.

—BRANDON KOSER
Grade 4

ROCKEFELLER
WILDLIFE PRESERVE:
MID-AUGUST

The air is moist
The water bittersweet
A southern Gulf breeze sighs
Laughing gulls call
And cicadas click their
Luminous song
I smell the death scent
Of beached gars
And see the dreamy haze
Of oil on water
Nearby an alligator stares
With tabby eyes
A great heron startles
From its marsh bed
Standing near the riprap,
I peer at the water
And slowly hoist

The turkey neck on string
A blue-point crab
Grips the bait
I slyly dip the net
A good two feet away
And scoop up the crustacean
Without warning
And drop it into the bucket
To meet many friends,
Gifts of the Mississippi
The day has reached its climax
Animals sleep in the heat,
Hiding in the wax myrtles
A snowy egret,
White plumage glistening,
Glides into the roseau cane.

—KEVIN MAHER
Grade 7

RAIN, THEN SUN

There are motions in the air
spiderwebs glisten
the creek swells
it is rain
then a gentle hum
the sky blooms
revealing the shy sun
a mosquito pierces the silence
into the cool, dark shade
then out to the blistering heat
seeking blood

—Daniel Chávez
Grade 5

BAYOU COTTAGE

Next to the muddy bayou, a sorry
excuse of an Acadian home.
Its broken swing dangles
from the porch ceiling.
Wildflowers and knee-high weeds
surround the shack.
Vines wind around large, worn supports.
In oversized, dirty clothes,
I gaze, watching the moss
drop to the ground
from a close-by cypress.
The stench of fish and mud
pollutes the air.
The sun hovers over the wet, exotic land,
shining on the gators below,
licking their lips with thoughts of
warm flesh between their teeth.

—GINNY MECHE
Grade 11

SUGAR AND RAIN

The dark skies
are a sign of the approaching beast.
The wind is opening
and slamming the screen door
repeatedly.
Clouds hang like curtains
over the humid air.

The storm is coming.

I can smell the rain.
Mama is standing on the porch in her apron.
I can tell she is worried because
the sky is far beyond gray,
and Papa hasn't come back from the barn yet.

The storm is coming.

I can see Papa's truck
coming down the dirt road.
He comes inside
just as the rain starts.
He is quiet.
I am sure his thoughts dwell
on the cane fields.

Mama
says there is no hope for them,
that once the hurricane passes,
there won't be much left.

The storm is coming.

Lightning crackles intermittently
casting eerie light
over the fields.
Mama is preparing dinner
and Papa is washing up.
My sisters and I are sitting in the living room,
quietly hoping
that our prayers for a miracle
will be answered.

The storm is here.

Rain pelts down
on the tin roof,
providing music for our silent dinner.
The stalks of cane
bow down to the horizon
under the weight of the wind.

The storm is here.

It is bedtime now.
I lie awake, listening to
the howls of that same beast
that turned the sky dark as night.
The rain is still falling.

The storm is here.

Morning—the rain has stopped,
and the wind
has died down.
Papa is out
surveying the damage dealt.
I can smell Mama's pancakes cooking.
My sisters are still asleep.

The storm has passed.

—ALYCE LABRY
Grade 9

RAINY DAY

As I sit on the porch,
I see the clouds low and gray,
gray as the tip of a pencil.
Then it starts to rain.

—CODY FONTENOT
Grade 8

LITTLE GREEN WORDS

As I write my poem under the sunset,
my green words come alive.
Although they are barefoot,
they run as fast as they can,
doing what, I don't know,
but now they dive into my picture
of a lake, then get out, dry off,
then turn back into my green words.

—SAM SUTHEIMER
Grade 6

INDEX OF POETS

ABOUT THE EDITOR

Poet and educator Sandy Lyne has taught poetry writing to more than forty thousand young people in grades three to twelve, and to several thousand teachers. He is a frequent presenter of workshops to teachers nationwide through his own Inner Writer Program and through the education programs of the John F. Kennedy Center for the Performing Arts. From 1993 to 1998, he helped design and presented a program to introduce poetry writing systemwide in the Lawrence, Kansas, schools. His own poems have appeared in numerous journals, including *The American Poetry Review, The Virginia Quarterly Review, Poetry East, Ploughshares, Louisiana Literature,* and *Louisiana Review,* and in two collections. He continues to give dozens of writing workshops each year to both teachers and students and to adults in retreat settings across the country. He now makes his home in Arnaudville, Louisiana.

For information on poetry-writing workshops write to:

Sandy Lyne
The Inner Writer Program
14 Hidden Hills Lake
Arnaudville LA 70512